Table of Contents

Inside maps and flags have been left blank so that the students may color them when they have completed the song. Refer to the cover for the appropriate colors.

©1993 by Hi. I. Que Publishing, P.O. Box 508,
Claremont, California 91711 • (909) 622-7501
International copyright secured.
All rights reserved.
Printed in U.S.A.

ISBN 0-9631333-3-0

Hi. I Que Publishing
Claremont, California 91711

Introduction

The purpose of this anthology is to provide students with access to National Anthems throughout the world.

Each country introduces it's children to their National Anthem early in life. Schools, parents and government are usually all involved in instilling pride in a child toward his/her own country.

It should be equally understood by all, that while there may be differences toward governments and cultures, people are inherently equal worldwide. Each person should be able to have pride for the soil on which they were born. Each person should be able to learn respect for another persons pride in their country.

One step in accomplishing this goal, hopefully, is to introduce the student to the anthems of other countries.

Through listening to the anthems of another country and giving thought to the words included, it is hoped that each person will become aware and learn to respect the pride another individual has toward their country.

We do hope that this education will help promote peace and respect among all.

BULGARIA

Form of Government: *National Assembly*

Predominant Language: *Bulgarian*

Capital: *Sofia*

Currency: *Lev*

National Holiday: *In transition*

NATIONAL ANTHEM OF BULGARIA:
MILA RODINO

(BULGARIAN)

GORDA STARA PLANEENA,
DO NEYEE DOONAVA SEENEYEE,
SLUNTSE TRAKEEYA OGRYAVA
NAD PEREENA PLAMENEYEE.

REFRAIN:
MEELA RODEENO,
(RODEENO),
TEE SEE ZEMEN RAYEE,
TVOYEETA HUBOST,
TVOYEETA PRELEST,
AH, TE NYAMAT KRAYEE!

NATIONAL ANTHEM OF BULGARIA:
OH, DEAR HOMELAND

(ENGLISH TRANSLATION)

PROUDLY SOAR THE BALKAN MOUNTAINS
AND BELOW THE DANUBE FLOWS;
OVER ALL THE SUN IS SHINING,
PIRIN STANDS IN PURPLE GLOW.

REFRAIN:
OH, DEAR HOMELAND,
(HOMELAND),
PARADISE ON EARTH!
FOR YOUR BEAUTY,
YOUR BEAUTY WILL FOREVER
CATCH OUR EYES.

National Anthem of Bulgaria
Mila Rodino

Words by
Tsvetan T. Radoslavov (1863-1931)

Melody by Tsvetan T. Radoslavov
Arranged by Kari H. Guthrie

FINLAND

Form of Government: *Republic*

Predominant Languages: *Finnish, Swedish*

Capital: *Helsinki*

Currency: *Markka*

National Holiday: *Independence Day - December 6th (1917)*

NATIONAL ANTHEM OF FINLAND: MAAMME LAULU - OUR LAND

(FINNISH)

OI MAAME, SUOMI, SYNNYNIMAA!
SOI SANA KULTAINEN!
EI LAAKSOA, EI KUKKULAA,
EI VETTA, RANTAA RAKKAAMPAA,
KUIN KOTIMAA TAA POHJOINEN,
MAA KALLIS ISIEN!

(ENGLISH TRANSLATION)

OUR LAND, OUR LAND, OUR FATHERLAND,
SOUND LOUD, O NAME OF WORTH!
NO MOUNT THAT MEETS THE HEAVEN'S BAND.
NO HIDDEN VALE, NO WAVEWASHED STRAND,
IS LOVED, AS IS OUR NATIVE NORTH.
OUR OWN FOREFATHERS' EARTH.

National Anthem of Finland
Maamme Laulu - Our Land

Words by
J.L. Runeberg (1804-1877)

Melody by Fredrik Pacius (1809-1891)
Arranged by Kari H. Guthrie

GREECE

Form of Government: *Republic*

Predominant Language: *Greek*

Capital: *Athens*

Currency: *Drachma*

National Holiday: *Independence Day - March 25th (1821)*

NATIONAL ANTHEM OF GREECE: ETHNIKOS HYMNOS

(GREEK)

SEGNOREES APO TIN KOPSI
TOO SPATHYOO TIN TROMERI;
SEGNOREES APO TIN OPSI
POO ME VYA METRA TIN YEE.
AP TA KOKKALA VYALMENEE
TON ELLEENON TA YE RA
KE SAN PRAWT' ANTHREEOMENEE
HYER'O HYERI ELEFTHERYA.
KE SAN PRAWT' ANTHREEOMENEE
HYER'O HYE R'ELEFTHERYA,
KE SAN PRAWT' ANTHREEOMENEE
HYER'O HYER' ELEFTHERYA.

NATIONAL ANTHEM OF GREECE: LIBERTY SONG

(ENGLISH TRANSLATION)

I SHALL ALWAYS KNOW YOU
BY THE TERRIBLE SWORD YOU HOLD,
AS THE WORLD, WITH SEARCHING VISION,
YOU SURVEY, WITH SUCH BOLD SPIRIT.
IT WAS THE ANCIENT GREEKS, WHOSE DEATH
BROUGHT THE BIRTH OUR FREE SPIRIT.
NOW, WITH ANCIENT BRAVERY RISING,
LET US GREET YOU, OH LIBERTY!
NOW, WITH ANCIENT BRAVERY RISING,
LET US GREET YOU, LIBERTY,
NOW, WITH ANCIENT BRAVERY RISING,
LET US GREET YOU, LIBERTY!

National Anthem of Greece
Ethnikos Hymnos - Liberty Song

Words by
Dionysis Solomos (1798-1857)

Melody by Nicholas Mantzaros (1795-1873)
Arranged by Kari H. Guthrie

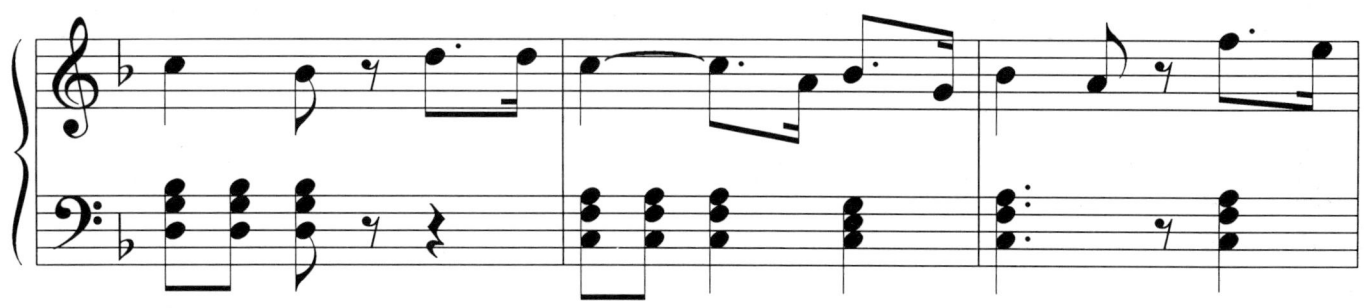

POLAND

Form of Government: *National Assembly*

Predominant Language: *Polish*

Capital: *Warsaw*

Currency: *Zloty*

National Holiday: *In transition*

NATIONAL ANTHEM OF POLAND: DABROWSKI'S MAZURKA

(POLISH)

JESZCZE POLSKA NIE
ZGINELA KIEDY MY ZYJEMY.
CO NAM OBCA PRZEMOC WZIELA
SZABLA ODBIERZEMY.

MARSZ, MARSZ, DABROWSKI,
Z ZIEMI WLOSKIEJ DO POLSKI!
ZA TWOIM PRZEWODEM,
ZLACZYM SIE Z NARODEM.

NATIONAL ANTHEM OF POLAND: DABROWSKI'S MAZURKA

(ENGLISH TRANSLATION)

POLAND WILL NOT BE LOST
UNTIL WE LIVE.
WE WILL FIGHT FOR EVERYTHING
THAT OUR ENEMIES
HAD TAKEN FROM US.

(CHORUS)
MARCH, MARCH DABROWSKI,
FROM ITALY TO POLAND!
UNDER YOUR COMMAND
WE WILL UNITE.

National Anthem of Poland
Dabrowski's Mazurka

Words by
Jozef Wybicki (1747-1822)

Melody: Folk Song
Arranged by Kari H. Guthrie

ROMANIA

Form of Government: *Republic*

Predominant Languages: *Romanian, Hungarian*

Capital: *Bucharest*

Currency: *Leu*

National Holiday: *In transition*

NATIONAL ANTHEM OF ROMANIA
DESTEAPTA-TE-ROMANE

(ROMANIAN)

DESTEAPTA-TE ROMANE
DIN SOMNUL CEL DE MAARTE
IN CARE TEADINCIRA
BARBARII DE TIRANI, BARBARII DE TIRANI!

(CHORUS)
ACUM ORI NICIODATA
CROIESTETI ALTA SOARTE,
LA CARE SA SENCHINE
SI CRUZII TAI DUSMANI, SI CRUZII TAI DUSMANI!
(REPEAT CHORUS)

(ENGLISH)

RISE YE, ROMANIAN
FROM THE SLEEP LIKE DEATH
IN WHICH YOU HAVE BEEN BOUND
BY THE SAVAGENESS OF TYRANNY,
SAVAGENESS OF TYRANNY!

(CHORUS)
NOW IS THE TIME
TO CREATE YOUR OWN DESTINY,
TO CAST OFF THE CHAINS OF
CRUELTY AND HATE, CRUELTY AND HATE!
(REPEAT CHORUS)

National Anthem of Romania
Desteapta-te-Romane

Words by
Andrei Muresan (19th Century)

Melody by Anton Pann
Arranged by Kari H. Guthrie

Maestoso

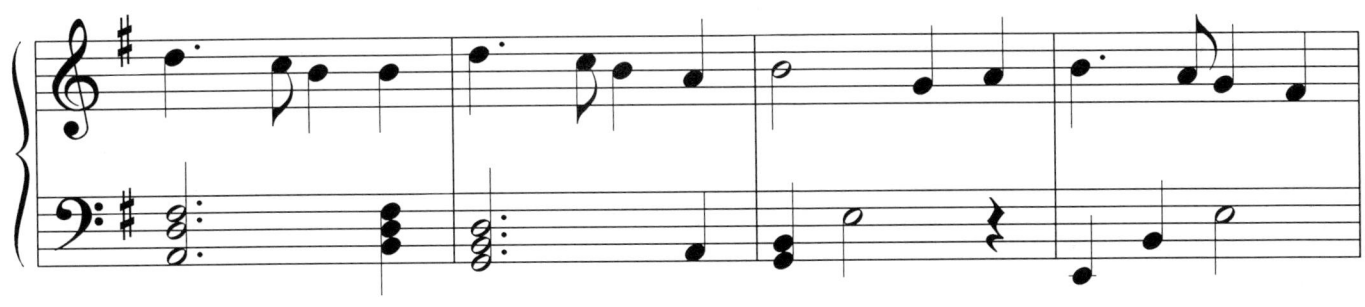

SOVIET UNION
(former)

Form of Government: *Federal Soviet Republic*

Predominant Languages: *Russian, other Slavik languages, Finno-ugric, Turkic and Mongol languages, Caucasian languages, Persian*

Capital: *Moscow*

Currency: *Ruble*

National Holiday: *The Great October Socialist Revolution - November 7th & 8th (1917)*

Note: *The Soviet Union dissolved in 1991. However, for historical interest we have supplied this information and anthem.*

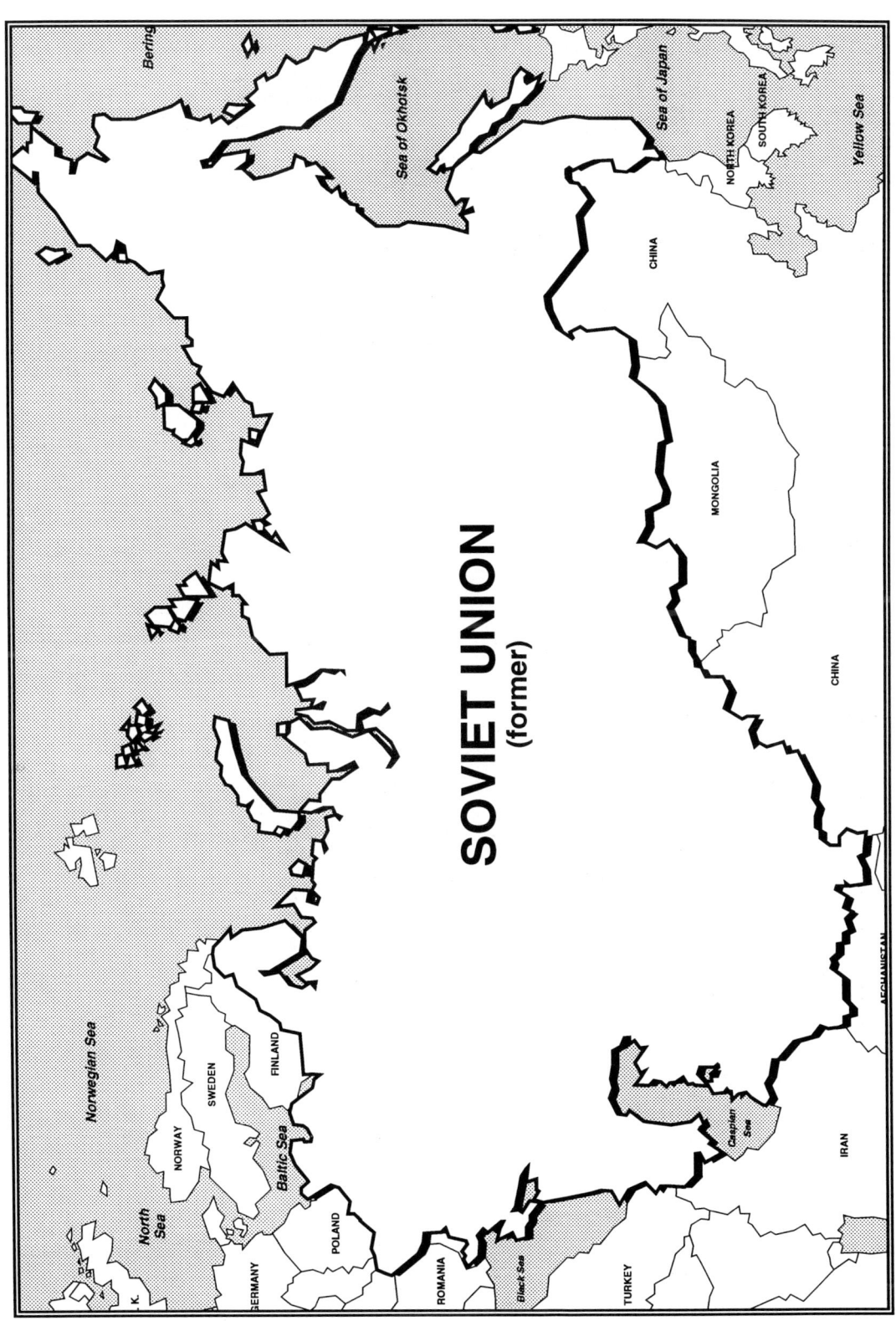

NATIONAL ANTHEM OF THE SOVIET UNION:
(former)

(RUSSIAN)

SOYUZ NERUSHIMI RESPUBLIK SVOBODNIKH
SPLOTILA NAVEKI VELIKAYA RUS'.
DA ZDRASTVUYET SOZDANNI VOLEI NARODOV,
YEDINI MOGUCHI SOVYETSKI!
SO YUZ!

(CHORUS)

SLAVSYA, OTYECHESTVO
NASHE SVOBOD NOYE,
DRUZHBI NARODOV NADYOZHNI OPLOT!
PARTIA LENINA,
SILA NARODNYAYA
NAS K TORZHESTVU KOMMUNIZMA VIDYOT!

NATIONAL ANTHEM OF THE SOVIET UNION:
(former)

(ENGLISH TRANSLATION)

UNBREAKABLE UNION
OF FREE-BORN REPUBLICS
GREAT RUSSIA HAS WELDED
FOR EVER TO STAND.
THY MIGHT WAS CREATED
BY WILL OF OUR PEOPLES,
NOW FLOURISH IN UNITY,
GREAT SOVIET LAND!

CHORUS

SING TO OUR MOTHERLAND,
HOME OF THE FREE,
BULWARK OF PEOPLES
IN BROTHERHOOD STRONG!
THE PARTY OF LENIN,
THE STRENGTH OF OUR PEOPLES,
TO COMMUNISM'S TRIUMPH LEAD US ON!

National Anthem of Soviet Union (former)

Words by
S. Mikhalkov (1913) & El-Reistan (1924)

Melody by A.V. Alexandrov (1883-1946)
Arranged by Kari H. Guthrie

YUGOSLAVIA

Form of Government: *Democracy*

Predominant Languages: *Serbo-Croatian, Slovenian,*
                                              Macedonian

Capital: *Belgrade*

Currency: *Dinar*

National Holiday: *In transition*

Note: *Prior to 1991 Yugoslavia included what is now Slovenia, Croatia, Bosnia, Hercegovina, Montenegro, Macedonia and Serbia. In April of 1992 Serbia and Montenegro formed a new smaller Yugoslavia.*

(1918 - 1991)

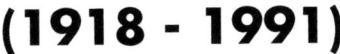

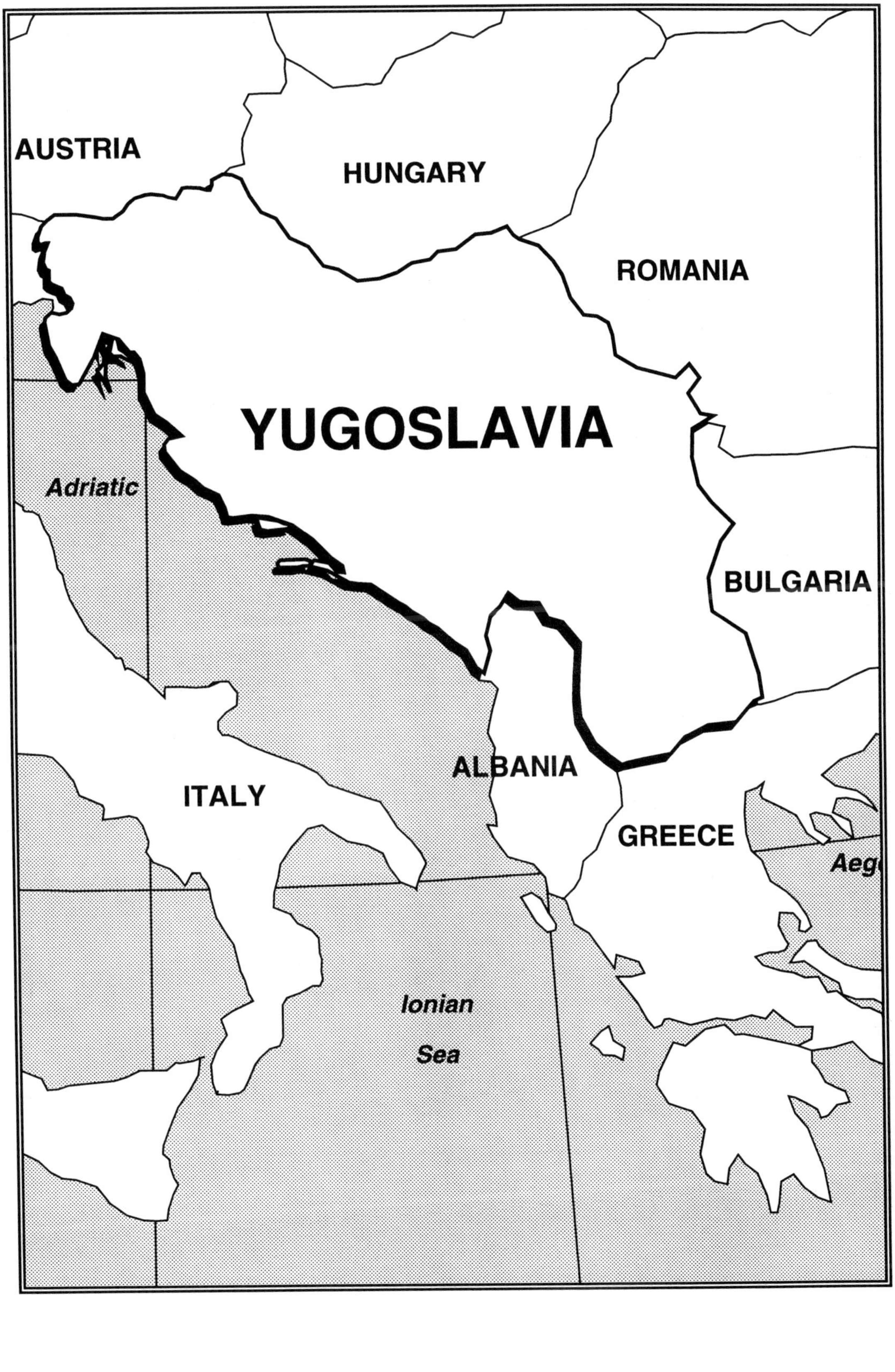
AUSTRIA
HUNGARY
ROMANIA
YUGOSLAVIA
Adriatic
BULGARIA
ALBANIA
ITALY
GREECE
Aeg
Ionian
Sea

(As of April 1992)

NATIONAL ANTHEM OF YUGOSLAVIA: HEJ SLOVENI

HEJ SLAVENI,
JOSTE ZIVI DUH NASIH DJEDOVA,
DOK ZA NAROD SRCE
BIJE NIJHOVIH SINOVA.
ZIVI, ZIVI, DUH SLAVENSKI
ZIVJET CES VJEKOVMA,
ZALUD PRIJETI PONOR
PAKLEA ZALUD VATRA GROMA.

(ENGLISH TRANSLATION)

FELLOW SLAVS,
THE SPIRIT OF YOUR ANCIENT BREED
STILL TRIUMPHS,
WHILE YOUR YOUTH STILL KNOWS
THE CAUSE OF THE WORKER AND THE PEASANT.
LONG TO LIVE SLAVONIC SPIRIT
THROUGH ALL THE COMING AGES.
IDLE THREATS OR HELL'S DEVICES,
IDLE FORCE OR TERROR.

National Anthem of Yugoslavia

Words by
Anonymous

Melody: Traditional
Arranged by Kari H. Guthrie